INVISIBLE ADVANTAGE
WORKBOOK

THE
INVISIBLE ADVANTAGE
WORKBOOK

TOM FORBES

Ghillie Suit Construction Made Simple

Also by Tom Forbes:

Invisible Advantage: A Step-by-Step Guide to Making Ghillie Suits
    and Custom Camouflage Clothing (video)
Modern Muzzleloading: Black Powder Shooting for Sport, Survival, & Self Defense (video)
More PVC Projects for the Outdoorsman: Building Inexpensive Shelters,
    Hunting and Fishing Gear, and More Out of Plastic Pipe
PVC Projects for the Outdoorsman: Building Shelters, Camping Gear,
    Weapons, and More Out of Plastic Pipe

The Invisible Advantage Workbook:
Ghillie Suit Construction Made Simple
by Tom Forbes

Copyright © 2002 by Tom Forbes

ISBN 13: 978-1-58160-310-1
Printed in the United States of America

Published by Paladin Press, a division of
Paladin Enterprises, Inc.
Gunbarrel Tech Center
7077 Winchester Circle
Boulder, Colorado 80301 USA
+1.303.443.7250

Direct inquiries and/or orders to the above address.

Visit our Web site at www.paladin-press.com

Table of
Contents

To Jill and Scout.
Thanks for all your hard work. Without your help, this would not have been possible.

WARNING

Do to the effectiveness and characteristics of the ghillie suit, neither the author nor Paladin Press accepts or claims responsibility for any accidents or injuries that may occur while using any of the projects or items described in this book. Whenever possible, use materials of a flame- or fire-resistant nature. Always treat materials with a quality flame or fire retardant prior to and after construction of any ghillie suit.

A bowhunter wears a ghillie suit in a wooded environment. To blend in with the leafy trees, he has added strips of burlap dyed a deep green, as well as bits of foliage.

Chapter 1

A Brief History
of the Ghillie Suit

ORIGINS

What is a ghillie suit?

It is basically a garment covered or garnished with strips and strands of cloth and vegetation that is used to camouflage or conceal the person wearing it. Ghillie suits can be made from jackets, shirts, ponchos, capes, or virtually any article of clothing. In this book, you will learn how to construct suits based on the popular battle dress uniform (BDU), ponchos, capes, and pants. The type of suit and the materials you use to construct a suit will depend on your individual needs. You will have many options from which to choose to help you construct a first-rate camouflage garment.

The ghillie suits is effective because it provides three-dimensional camouflage. Long before the use of printed camouflage patterns, soldiers and hunters learned the value of using simple burlap to help conceal themselves. The suit's varying colors create depth that replicates the randomness of nature, and the shaggy texture of the materials on the suit help break up the human silhouette. However, while the ghillie suit is effective in breaking up the human outline, it has the tendency to be rather bulky and warm to wear. Because of this, a ghillie suit should not be worn all the time. It is best to carry the suit in a rucksack or stash bag until needed for the stalk.

The suit took its name from some gamekeepers of Scotland, ghillies, a hardy breed of men who spent their lives in the Scottish Highlands stalking game, both two- and four-legged. They protected game and fish from unauthorized takers and served as guides for the landowners. Even though most ghillies were not landowners themselves, they refused to leave their beloved Highlands and move to more populated areas. They were true outdoorsmen, with intimate knowledge of the land.

Because their own survival depended on abundant game and fish, ghillies were protective of the local natural resources. Taking a very dim view of poachers, ghillies used every trick and tactic available to counter them—and one of the tricks was the ghillie suit.

MILITARY USE

The first recorded instance of a ghillie suit in military use was in World War I. Lord Lovat had commissioned a regiment, known as the Lovat Scouts, made up primarily of ghillies from the Highlands. Their purpose was, first, to use their marksmanship against the Germans, who had a clear advantage in this area because of their experienced hunters and *forstmeister* (forest rangers). Second, the ghillies were charged with training the largely urban-born British troops in the arts of observation and long-range shooting.

The ghillies brought with them their particular suits. The British War Ministry was so impressed with the garments that it set about creating its own kind of ghillie suit. The "issue" suit (as it was known) was effective, but was prone to snagging and catching on the vast amount of debris that littered no man's land.

Captain Herbert W. McBride, a veteran of the Great War, makes mention of these issue suits in his book, *A Rifleman Went to War*. McBride refers to them as "sniper robes" and comments on their being a hindrance in moving through no man's land. It should be noted, however, that the Allies were not the only ones to use ghillie suits. According Maj. H. Hesketh-Prichard's book, *Sniping in France*, both sides used a sniper's robe of some sort.

Following World War I ghillie suits, as well as whole sniping programs, fell into obscurity until the start of World War II. The ghillie suit was needed once again,

The British issue ghillie suit was very similar to the ones used on the other side of the battlefield (from The German Sniper 1914 – 1945 *by Peter R. Senich).*

and it was brought back into service by Allied armed forces. This is evident in the fact that British sniper manuals had written instructions on how to make a sniper suit. An excerpt from that manual is included in this book.

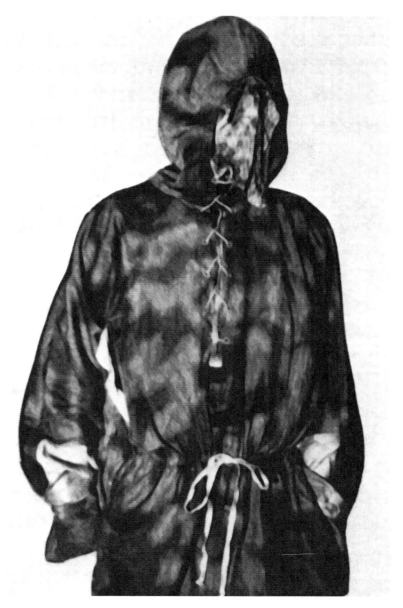

German camouflage smock (from The German Sniper 1914 – 1945*).*

After World War II, the sniper program and the ghillie suit again fell to the wayside. But the ghillie suit enjoyed renewed popularity in the United States in the early 1980s when the U.S. Marines adopted it for its snipers. Today, the ghillie suit is used by snipers and special operations units as well as elite law enforcement agencies.

Chapter 2

Ghillie Suit Construction

Construction must begin with the selection of a base garment. Selection criteria are needs, comfort, and climate. First, let's address needs. Do you need a suit that provides partial or full-body camouflage? Will a heavy suit restrict your movement? Will it be hot or cold in your area of operation?

The three base garments most commonly used in the construction of a ghillie suit are: coveralls, BDUs, and ponchos. All serve equally well, but you must decide which will work best for you. If you are making a simple camouflage hide, you may need just a large piece of netting.

> *When selecting netting, nylon cord is the best. It is more resistant to the elements and lasts longer. The netting squares should be no smaller than 3/4 inch and no larger than 2 inches. Squares that are too small make it difficult to thread the burlap strips and those that are too large create gaps in the garnish. Netting can be found in fabric and surplus stores.*

Coveralls, though providing the advantage of a one-piece base garment, tend to be too tight in the shoulders and thus make movement in the prone position somewhat difficult. Yes, you can use an oversized pair, but why do all the extra work if you don't have to? If you do use coveralls, I recommend removing the zipper and installing several buttons in its place. That way, if circumstances dictate getting out of the suit in a hurry, you can rip the buttons off and not worry about the zipper snagging or sticking.

Personally I prefer either BDUs or ponchos. BDUs work well for me because sometimes when hunting I don't always need full-body camouflage and will use the cammo jacket and hat with standard-issue pants. Ponchos are nice if I am in a stationary position and don't have to worry about them snagging on branches or cactus.

Here's a list of materials that you'll want to have on hand before you begin your project:

MATERIALS LIST

- Base garment
- Netting (preferably nylon type)
- Heavy thread or fishing line
- Large-gauge or heavy quilting needles
- Heavy scissors
- Stick pins
- Black marker
- Seam ripper or razor blade
- Strong glue, such as Tear Mender
- Glue gun
- Canvas or scraps of tire inner tube
- Camper's sleeping mat
- Burlap (old sandbags or seed bags, or burlap on the roll)
- Subdued-color or camouflage material
- Raffia (crating grass)
- Jute cord
- Hemp rope or twine
- Spray paint (subdued colors)
- Fabric dye
- Tagboard (heavy cardboard)
- Poster board
- Double-faced tape
- Buttoneer

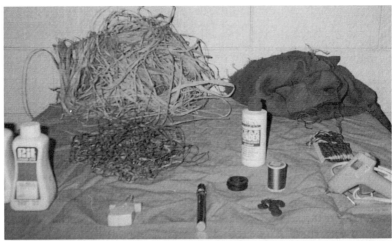

Materials for ghillie suit construction may include (top photo), clockwise from top right, burlap, nylon cord, a glue gun, buttons and thread, Tear Mender, waxed linen thread, heavy black marker, Buttoneer, fabric dye, nylon netting, and raffia. The bottom photo shows jute thread stripped from burlap material, raffia, heavy-gauge needles and thread, scissors, strong glue, and strips of burlap on canvas, plus a large piece of burlap draped over a camouflaged BDU base garment fitted with netting and canvas reinforcement.

THE BDU JACKET

Many ghillie suit makers begin by turning BDUs inside out so that they can still use the pockets. I do not do this. I keep the garment right side out and strip the pockets off the outside so that they don't interfere with the padding and reinforcement. If I feel the need I'll sew *one* to the inside of the jacket where I can get to it. It makes little or no sense to keep all the pockets because if you have to low crawl, the weight of your body will press on them and whatever is in the pocket is probably going to make you real uncomfortable.

Padding and Reinforcement

Padding, though not necessary, makes the suit much more comfortable. You can pad the primary contact points—knees, elbows, and chest—with 5/8-inch camping mat. This provides padding that will not absorb a lot of moisture. Over the top of the padding you can put canvas or heavy rubber, such as that found in truck tire inner tubes. You can secure these materials with carpet tape until they are sewed down.

Before you create the patterns for padding and reinforcement materials, you must have a way to keep your suit stretched out flat. You can make a quick form out of tagboard, a heavy, strong cardboard. Place the garment on top of the tagboard and pull it tight. Use pushpins to hold it in place or have someone help you hold it down while you trace the outline of the jacket using a felt-tip marker. Go seam

A BDU jacket with a padded and reinforced chest is pulled over a tagboard form. Netting has been attached and it is now ready to garnish.

to seam on each side and from the bottom hem to the seam at the top of the shoulders. Once this is done, remove the garment and cut out the pattern using heavy scissors or an X-ACTO or craft knife. Pull the garment over the form before proceeding.

Making Patterns

You need a separate pattern for each area of padding and reinforcement. The reinforcement material must overlap the padding, so you should make the reinforcement pattern out of poster board first.

Place the corner of the poster board at the bottom seam on the front of one side of the jacket. Use the

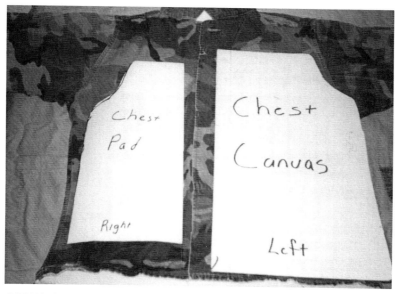

A BDU jacket on a tagboard form is shown with poster board patterns for padding and reinforcement.

seam that runs alongside the buttonholes as a guide on the edge of the board, but don't cover the buttonholes. Next, decide how high you want the canvas reinforcement to come on the jacket and draw a line there. Draw another line at the outside seam, making a rectangle. Cut it out. When you are done you should have a piece that covers the front of the jacket. If you want, you can remove the top outside corner of the pattern to create a pocket to seat the butt of a rifle. Base your padding pattern on these dimensions, shaving off about 2 inches in each direction.

If your base garment already has reinforced elbows, use the existing seams as a guide for making a padding pattern for them. Measure the dimensions of the reinforced elbow patch, transfer them to the pattern material, and cut out the pattern. Trace the pattern on your padding and cut it out. Once the padding is cut to shape, make a slit in the top seam in the reinforcement above the elbow and slide the padding in. If your base garment does not have reinforced elbows, you can easily make a pattern for them by adding two inches to the dimensions of the padding pattern. Cut out the pattern and trace it onto the canvas. Cut out the reinforcement material, place a strip of double-faced tape on it, and lay the canvas over the padding. It is ready to be sewn down.

Attaching the Material

Sewing can be accomplished by two methods. You can do it by hand or take the jacket to a canvas or saddle shop and have it done on one of their heavy-duty sewing machines. The cost is usually only a couple of dollars and it saves many hours of fighting with a needle and thread (there will be plenty of opportunities for that). An alternative to sewing is using strong glue to attach the padding and reinforcement. This will work, but is not quite as durable as sewing.

Dealing with Heat

Before attaching the netting and garnish, you may want to make some alterations. Warm weather and ghillie suits do not go well together because ghillie suits tend to be heavy and very hot. One way to make the suit more user-friendly is to remove the material from the

A large rectangle has been cut out of the back of this BDU jacket. The section will be replaced with netting to help keep the finished suit cool.

center of the back and replace it with mesh or mosquito netting. This will help the suit breathe. The same can be done to the top of the hat or hood and even the areas under the arms on a jacket or the inseam of the legs on a pair of pants.

To replace a portion of the back with mesh or mosquito netting to allow body heat to escape, sew a whipstitch at each square along the seams on both sides and at the top of the shoulders. Don't sew the netting along the bottom hem because the netting will stretch and gather weight, causing a lump in the garnish. It is best to let it hang loose for two reasons: (1) it allows the garnish to hang over the top of the pants and (2) if the suit gets wet you can slide cardboard spacers under the netting to allow air to circulate and speed up drying.

This is also a good time to sew a canteen or Camelbak water bag into the back or under the arm of your jacket. You can then run a rubber drink tube up to the collar to give you access to hydration in an arrangement that won't cause unnecessary movement.

Netting

Before securing the netting to the garment, the netting must be cut to size. Place the netting over the jacket, which is held rigid with the tagboard form.

Place the netting over the shoulders of the jacket, lining up the netting with the outside seams. Pin or tack the netting in place along the seams, making sure that you have the same number of squares on both sides of the neck. It is best to use separate pieces of netting on

The netting has been secured, and this BDU jacket is ready for garnish.

each side of the collar on the front of the suit: this helps relieve the pressure on the shoulders caused by the weight of the garnish. The garnish on the front should come down 6 to 8 inches, or to the old seam on the top pocket. The netting should not go to past the elbow on either sleeve. The garnish can be tied long enough to hang down to the hands.

There are several ways to attach the netting to the base garment. You can sew the netting on with heavy fishing line or waxed linen thread using a large quilting needle or canvas sewing needle. Before sewing the netting down, I use a Buttoneer to tack the netting in place. Once the netting is in place, I cut it to fit the garment, and then sew it down along the outside edge.

If I am covering a large area, such as a poncho or the back of BDU jacket, I sew random stitches across the area to help hold the netting in place. (This is best done after the garment is garnished. If done right away the garnish has a tendency to pucker.)

The netting can also be attached to the base garment with glue. This is done by simply laying the netting over the base garment and gluing the netting down at various points. When the glue has dried, trim away the excess netting.

Another way to attach the netting is to sew buttons to the base garment, then attach loops to the netting to hook around the buttons. This may take longer, but it allows you to remove the netting and wash the base garment, or even to change the garnish to suit a change in the environment.

A close-up of garnish attached to nylon netting shows that simple knots are all you need.

A basic quilter's rack is handy for holding garments while you work on them.

Garnish

Now comes the fun part. Begin taking strips of garnish and tying them to the netting. You will be able to work more freely and see what you are doing if you start at the bottom and work your way up the jacket, in the same manner as shingling a roof.

Garnish can be strips of camouflaged or subdued-color cloth, burlap, or crafting raffia. Burlap can be scrounged from many different sources, such as old gunnysacks or sandbags. Some fabric shops and craft shops even carry it on rolls, which could save you a lot of time.

Jute cord is quicker to work with than burlap fabric: just cut it to length and attach it to the netting. While this is definitely faster in terms of construction, it is also more expensive. The decision is yours; both will create a great suit. The colors can be changed with common fabric dyes, but in many cases you may be better off just using your chosen material's natural color. To make garnishing the suit easier I use what I like to call "the rack." A rack designed for quilters will hold the garment steady in front of you while you are working. It is also adjustable in height, which is a real benefit when you start tying garnish onto the suit.

Determining color is best done by taking a color photo of the general area in which you intend to be operating. Study the picture to pick out what the predominant colors are to help you create a more effective suit. If there was only one color that I could go with, it would be the natural dusty-brown color of burlap. Remember, no

The author wears a ghillie suit made with heavy, wide strips of burlap to replicate broadleaf vegetation. Notice how he uses the shadows of the foliage to help conceal himself.

matter how much garnish you use, the suit is made more effective by adding natural vegetation.

When tying the strips, a simple knot will work just fine. I have found that shorter strips tend to stand up and longer ones tend to lie down. I use the shorter strips on the back and use the longer ones on the sides where they drape over, concealing the sides. An alternative to using strips of burlap is to use individual *strands* of burlap. This is done by pulling the individual strands from the material and then tying small bundles of 8 to 10 strands to the netting. This is very time-consuming, but creates an awesome effect.

Remember to not use too much of a particular color in the same area, and to avoid very dark colors. True black rarely appears in nature; stick to subdued tones and spread out the colors.

One more option you might consider for the jacket is to alter it to keep the sleeves from riding up on your arms while you are crawling. There are two ways to do this. One is to sew a loop of parachute cord to the cuff near your thumb. Make it long enough to loop over your thumb to hold the sleeve down on the wrist. The other way is to sew a strip of material across the opening in the sleeve at the cuff: this strip should be centered to cross the palm over the web of the hand.

Above: This finished ghillie suit will be used for bowhunting, so the left side has been left ungarnished to prevent the bowstring from snagging. The back of the suit is fully garnished, including raffia.

Opposite page: The raffia-garnished ghillie suit blends seamlessly into the waving prairie grass, giving this bowhunter the concealment he needs.

Patterns for padding and canvas reinforcement are shown on a pair of BDU pants.

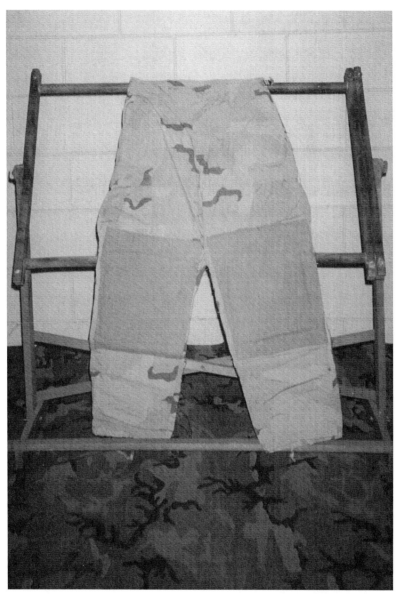

With the knees padded and reinforced, the BDU pants are secured to the rack.

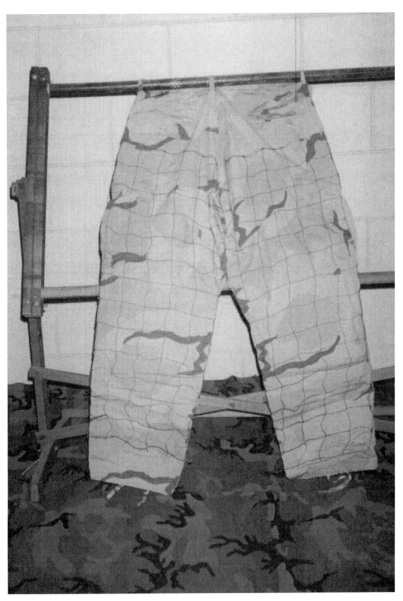

With the netting attached (above), the BDU pants are ready for garnishing (right).

THE BDU PANTS

With the jacket complete you can start on the pants. Padding and canvas reinforcement for the knees are done in the same manner as the elbows on the jacket. The netting is attached from seam to seam, but does not go all the way to the top of the pants (I usually stop below the back pockets). There is little need to go higher than the pockets since a jacket and the garnish from it will more than likely hang over the top of the pants. Also, I rarely run the netting to the bottom hem of the pants, for if the garnish is tied long there is no need. This can save you some time and work.

BDU pants, when fully garnished and padded, do get heavy and have a tendency to want to fall down. You can use a belt, but if you cinch it up too tight it can become very uncomfortable. So I recommend using suspenders. There are a couple of different ways to do this. The first is a field-expedient method. Take a set of military-issue suspenders and run the hooks through the waist adjustment tabs. Another quick method is to take parachute cord, make a loop with it, and tie it to the top of the belt loops. If time allows, these loops can also be sewn to the top of the pants.

The more traditional way is to sew buttons to the top of the pants and then to attach a pair of suspenders to them. Suspenders used for fishing waders work real well and are not very expensive.

An alternative to using suspenders is to sew a button to the top of the back of the BDU pants. Then the button tab is cut from the side of a BDU jacket and sewn to the inside of the jacket just above the where the waistline is when the BDU pants are worn. (To figure where to put the tab, bend over while wearing the pants and jacket, and have someone mark where the button is to go.) Once the tab is secured, just button the jacket to the pants and you have it.

Leggings

An alternative to doing a pair of pants is to make a pair of leggings or chaps. Construction is similar to that of the pants, but it goes a little quicker. On the leggings, the netting is secured at the top and from seam to seam like the pants. Leggings can be made from a pattern purchased from a fabric shop or made from an old pair of pants by cutting the legs somewhere between the knees and the bottoms of the back pockets. Sew a loop to the outside of the leggings. This loop needs to be long enough to reach the belt line because a belt is used to hold the leggings up. After this is done, attach the netting and garnish.

Gaiters

Camouflaged leg gaiters offer a handy alternative for people who don't need or want to go through the work of making a pair of pants. The gaiters can be made from a pair of gaiters purchased at an outdoor or military surplus store.

The gaiters are quick and easy to make. Simply wrap the netting around the gaiters, then sew it into place and tie on the garnish.

This finished ghillie suit (above), complete with padded and reinforced chest, knees, and elbows, plus garnish, is based on a hunting suit. It stands out clearly against a dark, flat background, but when used in a prairie environment where it matches the color and texture of its surroundings (opposite page), it virtually disappears.

A completed gaiter and one with the netting attached, ready to be garnished.

HEADGEAR

Without a doubt, the best way to hide one's face is to use a camouflage face paint of some sort. But for those who don't want to mess with paint, the best option is a hat, face mask, or hood. There are many different types available for purchase, but here are a couple of different coverings you can make for yourself.

Hat

The hat is fairly simple to make. Start by laying a piece of netting over a boonie or floppy hat. Your hat does not necessarily need to be this style; a baseball cap will work but does not break up your outline as well. If

A finished ghillie hat (left) and one with netting attached, waiting for garnish.

you wish to make the hat a little cooler, cut a 4-x-4-inch square out of the top. Then sew or glue a piece of mesh or mosquito netting in its place.

With the netting laid out you have the option of putting a veil on the hat. It can hang down to cover your face, or can be made longer to stretch out and cover a camera or rifle scope. A long veil will allow you to manipulate such items with the movement being concealed.

Attach the netting by tacking it down to the front of the brim and working toward the back. Once it is attached to the brim, secure it to the crown of the hat. Allow the excess netting to hang a foot or so past the back of the brim, overlapping the jacket. Once the netting is secured, begin garnishing the hat.

35

From top right a finished hat, a cammo face mask, a winter-white face mask, and a store-bought white ski mask.

Equipment such as spotter scopes and range finders that won't be covered by a veil can be camouflaged by wrapping them with strips of burlap. After wrapping the burlap, secure the loose ends with green duct tape (known in the military as "hundred-mile-an-hour tape"). Also, you can make your own camouflage tape by applying spray-on adhesive to one side of the burlap strips.

Face Mask

The face mask is very simple to construct. It can be made from an old BDU top, or a plain white pillowcase should you have need for winter camouflage.

A German soldier wears burlap sacking over his helmet (from The German Sniper 1914 – 1945*).*

First, take a piece of string and hold one end below your left ear. Then bring the string across your nose to your right ear and mark the length. Use this length of string to determine the width of the mask. Now measure from the top of your nose to the center of your chest to give you the length of the mask, which you will want long enough that it can be tucked into your jacket. Now, take a piece of string or bootlace and lay it across the top of the material. Roll the material down so that the string is held within the rolled material. Here you can do one of two things: either sew the rolled material down or glue it with fabric glue. Once this is done your mask is complete. If you are so inclined, make it reversible by having BDU material on one side and sewing or gluing white material on the other, thus providing one mask to serve two environments.

Hood

A hood can be constructed almost as easily as the face mask, and again you have the option of making it reversible. The easiest and quickest method for making a hood is to simply cut the hood off an old BDU field jacket. If you wish to make a hood more suited to your needs, this old field jacket hood will provide a good pattern. Another source for a hood is the trusty army surplus store where you can find old parka hoods, which work well once they have had all their insulation removed, and they make great patterns, too. Attach the hood with buttons to make it removable.

A poncho-based ghillie suit with a drawstring is worn with a garnished hat.

A hunter wearing a poncho-based ghillie suit settles into the shadows at the base of a tree. The barrel of his rifle is wrapped in burlap to help camouflage it.

THE PONCHO

Poncho-based ghillie suits are rather easy to construct. You can either purchase a poncho and attach the netting and garnish it as we have done with the jacket, or you can make your own poncho from scratch.

To make your own poncho, start with at least two yards of cloth and fold it in half. Sew the sides together leaving an opening at the top of each side for arm holes.

This poncho-based ghillie suit has been garnished front and back.

Then cut a hole in the center of the fold for your head. It is wise to reinforce the neck by sewing another piece of cloth around the hole, which will give it the strength needed to support the heavy garnish.

You'll also want to install a drawstring around the waist. This will serve two purposes: it will help to keep wind from coming up through the garment, and it will relieve some of the weight of the garnish.

The netting is attached in the same manner as the

Whenever possible use a base garment made of the fire-resistant material Nomex. Flight suits and some BDUs are made of this material. Ghillie suits, by their shaggy nature, can be prone to catching fire. Be sure to treat the base garment and the garnish with a good fire retardant. **This is very important.** *Never wear a ghillie suit near fire or flame and stay away from machinery or moving parts.*

netting on the jacket, reaching from seam to seam and going over the top of the shoulders and down the front. I do not normally put a hood on a poncho because then it can't be turned around and used along with the garnish in the front. This is really handy for hunting turkeys or when you are sitting with your back to a tree or fence post. The same holds true for hunting waterfowl in decoys. It allows you to lie on your back with the garnish covering your front.

CONSTRUCTING A QUICK CAPE

The quick cape is a great alternative garment for the individual who wants maximum camouflage but does not need full body cover. Since the cape covers only the head and shoulders, it is best used in circumstances where most of the body is hidden, as in using a hunting blind or in conducting surveillance from a spider hole. The quick cape can be constructed in a matter of hours with a minimum amount of materials.

MATERIALS LIST

- A large burlap bag
- Two or 3 yards of burlap
- Waxed linen thread
- Large-gauge needle
- Scissors
- Hot-glue gun
- Elastic

Begin by cutting the burlap bag in half width-wise. Then cut one of the halves in half again. You will use one of the corners for the hood.

To create the hood you must first fix it to accept a drawstring. This can be done two different ways. You can (1) sew a strip of seam tape around the opening for the face, or (2) take a piece of tape and lay it an inch back from the edge of the face and then roll it back and tack it in place with the hot-glue gun. Once the tape is in place, sew it down. The tape is there to help prevent the glue from seeping through and closing up the draw-string. By doing this, the drawstring should slide freely.

When you have finished the hood, find the center of the body of the cape and cut it down the center the distance that the hood is deep. Insert the hood into the

THE SMOCK

THE HOOD

PAINTING A SNIPER SUIT

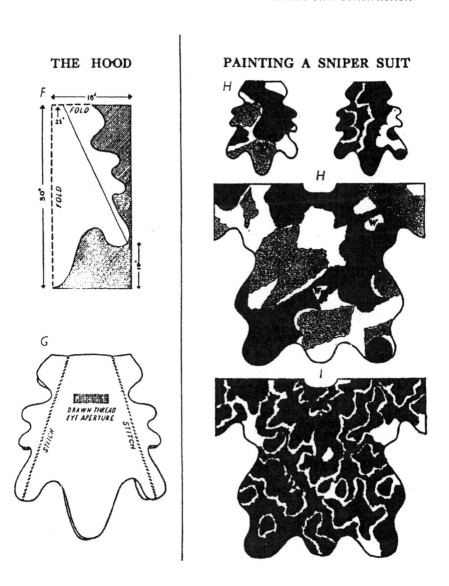

These drawings for a ghillie suit "smock" and hood were issued to members of the British military forces during World War II. The simple design holds up to this day.

> *One of the best accessories you can add to any suit is a hydration system. Military 2-quart canteens work well with drinking tube, but I feel the best is a Camelbak or similar hydration system. If the system is installed in the back or the side of the suit, the wearer can run the drink tube up to where it can be used without a lot of unnecessary movement.*

opening and hot-glue it to the burlap bag, letting about 3 inches of hood overlap the body of the cape. Using the waxed linen thread, sew the hood in place.

Begin cutting the extra pieces of burlap and laying them over the shoulders and back of the cape. Do one piece at a time, gluing or stitching them to the base of the cape, then whip-stitching them into place. Once the pieces are secured you can either cut the burlap into strips or fray it into individual threads—whichever you prefer. Continue to build on each layer until you achieve the desired results. When the base is finished, go to the top of the hood and do the same thing with the pieces of burlap. Secure the pieces of burlap with glue or by sewing, then cut them into strips or fray them into individual strands. Make sure that the pieces drape at least to the shoulders; a couple of inches past is even better.

If the drawstring on the hood is not adequate to hold the cape in place, attach an elastic strip from the front to the back under each arm. These straps can be slipped under the arms and will help to hold the cape in place if the wearer needs to move.

THE BRITISH MILITARY SNIPER SUIT

During World War II, the British government published a pamphlet, *Notes on the Training of Snipers: Military Training Pamphlet No. 44—1940.* Contained within are detailed instructions for sniper training, including sections on fieldcraft, sniping in open warfare, and sniping from houses and buildings. Appendices include notes on range practices, panoramic drawing, and methods of locating enemy snipers. Most interesting for our purposes is Appendix 9: Sniper Suits.

A copy of the manual was provided by a friend who accurately predicted that I would find it very helpful. As I stated before, construction of the suit is very easy and could easily be finished in an hour or two.

MATERIALS LIST

- Three yards of burlap (cut into three 1-yard pieces)
- Needles
- Thread
- Hot-glue gun
- Half a yard of canvas
- A drawstring

Front and back views of the British sniper suit with hood. The sides will be stripped and frayed to resemble grass. This suit could be painted or dyed.

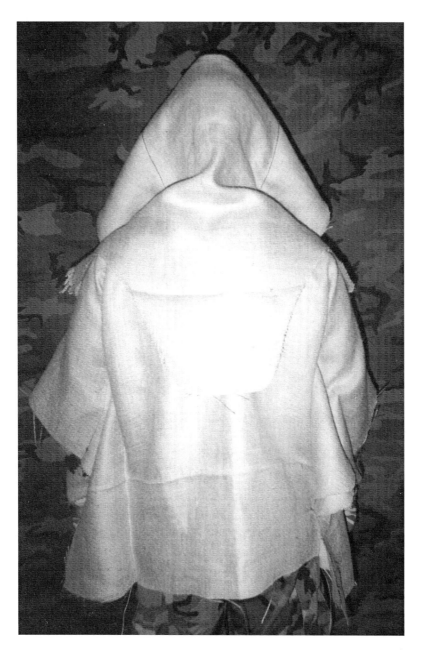

Here the British sniper suit is shown with the edges cut into strips to further break up its outline.

Begin by folding two of the pieces as shown in the illustration on p. 44, making sure the edges line up. Then draw the outline of the suit with chalk and cut it out. Stitch any pockets to either the inside or the outside of the garment. (Pockets sewn on the inside will require that a slit be cut in the front of garment. Be sure to sew a hem into the slit to prevent its fraying.) Once you have sewn the pocket, sew a flap over it to prevent debris from entering it.

Now sew the front of the garment to the back. Use a heavy thread and, if time permits, double-stitch the seams. If you are looking to put together a quick suit that will not see heavy use or extreme cold, you can get by using the hot-glue gun instead of needle and thread.

Roll down a 1-inch wide flap and tack it in place and insert the neck drawstring. Then sew it down. Once the suit is done, you can either leave the irregular outline of the suit, cut the edges into strips, or fray the burlap into individual strands. It depends on personal taste and the terrain in which you'll be operating.

To make the hood, take the remaining yard of burlap, fold it over, draw the outline, and cut it out. Determine the center of the hood and cut the eye aperture. This should be roughly 1 inch wide by 6 inches long. A suggestion is to place seam tape around the opening, which helps prevent fraying plus giving clearer vision. With the hood complete, the decision to fray it or leave it is up to you.

Options

The British military sniper suit is very nice because it may be constructed as a basic garment or may be enhanced by adding such extras as a liner or multiple pockets. Sewing loops using simple whip-stitches will allow for attaching vegetation. Also, if you so desire, canvas can be used to reinforce the elbows and bottom front portion of the smock. There are a number of options for color schemes: burlap with a camouflage print can be used, or you can create your own. Where I live the terrain is mostly prairie and, by using the right shade of burlap, I can get by without any additional colors. To add more depth to the suit, take the remaining strands of burlap that you have from stripping and latch-hook them into the smock and hood.

WINTER GHILLIE SUIT

Probably the most overlooked environment when one thinks of ghillie suits is the winter landscape. A winter ghillie suit is easy to make and will greatly enhance your ability to be undetected in snow-covered terrain.

Most camouflage for snow consists of a simple white garment or coveralls. (Those that have additional colors tend to overdo it.) To construct a winter suit, simply begin with a set of coveralls or even a plain white poncho.

Attach strands of burlap or, as I prefer, strands of raffia. Attach the strands randomly and sparsely. You want to replicate the look of dead grass and other vegetation sticking up through the snow.

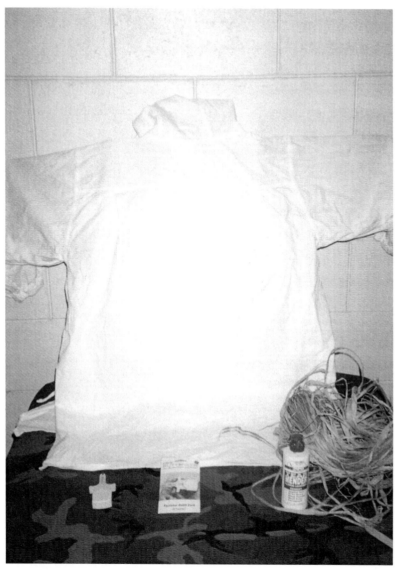

Constructing a winter ghillie suit is a bare-bones project. All you'll need is a white or light-colored base garment, some raffia, glue, and perhaps a Buttoneer or a large sewing needle.

Now you see him . . .

. . . now you don't.

The strands can be attached by sewing them to the garment or by using fabric cement or glue. If the base garment is burlap, hot glue works very well and is surprisingly durable. Another method is to sew long strands of burlap or jute cord directly into the base garment and to leave the ends hanging down. This is done simply by using a large needle and pushing it through the base garment and pulling it out. Pull the strand of raffia or burlap about halfway through, remove the needle, and tie a knot so the strand of garnish will not back out or come loose.

Chapter 3

Making a Drag Bag

A drag bag is a garnished gun case that can pulled or dragged behind you as you crawl along the ground. It can be made from an existing gun case or built to suit your needs. If you are going to use an existing gun case, all you have to do is to attach the netting from seam to seam just like the garments we have shown and then attach the garnish. However, before attaching the netting it would be wise to secure a length of heavy cord or a strap to the case and then attach it to your ghillie suit. This can be done by using a snaplink that hooks to a ring attached to the middle or the back of your suit. This allows you to keep your hands free while crawling.

Making a drag bag isn't that difficult.

MATERIALS LIST

- Two pieces of canvas or heavy camouflage material 2 1/2 feet wide by 5 feet long
- Two pieces of camping mat 1 foot wide by 4 1/2 feet long
- One piece of canvas 1 foot wide by 8 inches long
- One 6-inch length of parachute cord or webbing
- One snaplink
- Netting and garnish

Follow the diagrams shown in Figures 3-1 through 3-3.

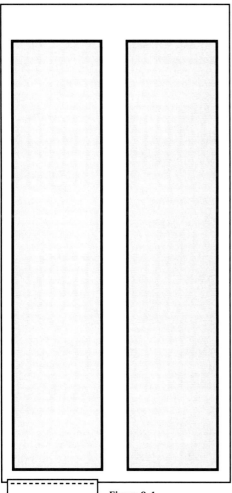

Figure 3-1.

    Begin by laying out one 2 1/2-x-5-foot piece of canvas. Place the 1-foot-x-8-inch piece near a corner and sew it to the canvas as shown. This small piece will be the flap for the open end. At the opposite end, sew down the cord or webbing.

    Place a piece of matting on the material, 1 inch up from the bottom of the material and 1 inch in from the edge. Now, do the same on the other side of the material. Use double-faced tape to hold the padding and material in place.

Figure 3-2.
With the matting in place, lay the second piece of canvas over the top of the matting. Sew the top and bottom together on the outside of the matting. Then sew down the center, top to bottom.

Figure 3-3.
Fold the material lengthwise and sew the bottom and open edge closed. Sew or glue the netting and garnish.

Chapter 4

Stalking

Stalking, by its simplest definition, is the ability to get as close as possible to an intended target without being detected. Obviously, there is more to conducting a successful stalk than just being well camouflaged. Stalking is as much an art as it is a skill. To be good at stalking requires patience, endurance, and a healthy dose of instinct. To bring these attributes together requires practice.

Of the three requirements the hardest for those of us in modern society is patience. We live in a world filled with vast amounts of stimuli that provide us with instant gratification, something not at all related to patience.

We have to teach ourselves to move just a little slower or wait just one more minute—not an easy task when the adrenaline is running high or boredom has overtaken us. Impatience will cause us to act rashly, without thought or regard for our actions. Such activity more often than not results in failure. By being patient, we can slow things down to see them more clearly and look at them with greater objectivity.

The first consideration when planning a stalk is to know your intended target—is it man or beast? If it is man, the first consideration is whether he is a physical threat to you. If any threat exists you will obviously have to use extreme caution. This is also true if stalking dangerous or wounded game.

If dealing with man, some questions that should be answered are these: What is the background of this person? Has he had any military or law enforcement training? Does he have an urban or rural background? What is his age and health? What is his motivation? In addition, a very important consideration is whether he is in an area familiar to him.

In stalking wild game the questions obviously change, but exist nonetheless. What is the game you are stalking? What do its tracks and droppings look like? Is the animal wounded or healthy? Is it in an area frequented by people? Is it used to people? What are its habits? What is the terrain? Where is the heaviest cover or water?

As a soldier or hunter alien to a particular area of operation, you can do much to get a feel for the land. Learn how to use topographical maps and photos. Simply talk to locals about the terrain and learn the significant landmarks.

THE STALK

Make sure you have the right ghillie suit or camouflage for your environment. You have to decide whether you need a full ghillie suit or can get by with a quick cape or a simple, garnished cover. (Remember, a full ghillie suit can get awfully warm.) Make sure that all your gear is secured and quiet; tape down anything that is loose and makes noise while you are moving, such as a camera or gunsling, and don't let items brush against one another.

Check your footgear. Is it hard- or soft-soled? Tennis shoes can be real handy for stalking and a good pair of moccasins is hard to beat. For hard-soled boots, provided the terrain is agreeable, slip an oversized pair of wool socks over the outside. This will help to muffle your footfall. Heavy felt liners can be modified to fit over the soles of a pair of boots—but be careful because if the liners get wet they can be very slippery.

Walking

When stalking one should walk as if on eggshells. I often think of the cartoons where the wolf is sneaking through the forest on its tiptoes. This may be a bit of stretch, but not much. Walk toes first, followed by the side of the foot, then the heel, and last the ball. This allows you to control the amount of pressure you put on the ground. Plan the next step before you take it. Look where you will place your foot. Avoid leaves and twigs; step *over* logs, not *on* them—they may be rotten and could break with a crash at the slightest pressure.

Learn to walk with the wind. I don't mean walk with the wind at your back, I mean use the wind to help cover your movement. This does two things; it allows the wind to help cover any sound you make and it puts your body in motion when other things are being moved by the wind. This is easy to do. First, listen for the gust to come up. You will usually hear it before you feel it. When you see things around you begin to move, that's when you move. As the gust subsides, prepare to stop. By preparing to stop you allow yourself the opportunity to be in a natural and comfortable position to wait for the next gust. Your legs and back can cramp up pretty fast if you are not comfortable.

The 10-by-10 Method of Walking

The 10-by-10-step method was something I stumbled across years ago while bowhunting white-tailed deer. You simply take 10 steps and stop, then look from side to side as far as your head will turn and count to yourself "one-one thousand, two-one thousand," and so on until you reach 10. Once you are sure that you have seen all there is to see, take the next steps and start all over again. This is slow movement, but it pays off.

When moving in hilly terrain it is best to stop well

below the crest and crawl up to the top. Avoid silhouetting yourself. Remember, look *around* objects, not over them, whenever possible.

Another method of walking is what I call "deer walking." This is used in hilly or uneven terrain when I want to move a little faster. If you have ever seen how deer walk over the top of a hill you will know exactly what I'm talking about. As you approach the crest of a hill, stop just below it where you can begin to see over the top. Then take a step and look side to side using the 10 count. Then take the next step and continue to look using the 10 count. Do this until you have reached the crest.

Keep cover between you and your target. This may be a tree, a fence, or even a small bush. Use every bit of available cover. Depressions and low spots should be used whenever possible. The only drawback to this, if you wish to call it one, is that wildlife use these same depressions and low spots.

When moving in wooded or jungle terrain, make use of shadows and avoid walking where the sun shines through the leaves, which would be like walking in a spotlight.

Finally, any good soldier will tell you to stay off trails, which may be revealed by breaks in foliage, beaten or disturbed soil, or even a lack of spider webs. Try to move parallel to trails whenever possible, and take advantage of any cover and concealment you can—especially with a ghillie suit.